Map Workbook

for

WESTERN CIVILIZATION:

VOLUME 2: Since 1300

Map Workbook
for

WESTERN CIVILIZATION:

VOLUME 2: Since 1300

Cynthia Kosso
Northern Arizona University

West/Wadsworth
I⊤P® An International Thomson Publishing Company

Belmont, CA • Albany, NY • Boston • Cincinnati • Johannesburg • London • Madrid • Melbourne
Mexico City • New York • Pacific Grove, CA • Scottsdale, AZ • Singapore • Tokyo • Toronto

Cover Image: *Many Happy Returns of the Day* (detail), by William Powell Frith (1819-1909); by permission of Harrogate Museums and Art Gallery, North Yorkshire, UK; Bridgeman Art Library, London/New York.

Printed in Canada.
  2 3 4 5 6 7 8 9 10

For more information, contact Wadsworth Publishing Company, 10 Davis Drive, Belmont, CA 94002, or electronically at http://www.wadsworth.com.

International Thomson Publishing Europe
Berkshire House
168-173 High Holborn
London, WC1V 7AA, United Kingdom

International Thomson Editores
Seneca, 53
Colonia Polanco
11560 México D.F. México

Nelson ITP, Australia
102 Dodds Street
South Melbourne
Victoria 3205 Australia

International Thomson Publishing Asia
60 Albert Street #15-01
Albert Complex
Singapore 189969

Nelson Canada
1120 Birchmount Road
Scarborough, Ontario
Canada M1K 5G4

International Thomson Publishing Southern Africa
Building 18, Constantia Square
138 Sixteenth Road, P.O. Box 2459
Halfway House, 1685 South Africa

International Thomson Publishing Japan
Hirakawa-cho Kyowa Building, 3F
2-2-1 Hirakawa-cho
Chiyoda-ku
Tokyo 102, Japan

Senior Developmental Editor: Sharon Adams Poore
Editorial Assistant: Melissa Gleason
Ancillary Coordinator: Rita Jaramillo
Print Buyer: Judy Inouye

ISBN 0-534-56082-2

VOLUME TWO
TABLE OF CONTENTS

CHRONOLOGIES

1. Europe: AD 1000-1600
2. Early Modern Europe: AD 1600-1800
3. Modern Europe: AD 1800 to the Present

INTRODUCTION

Map reading is an important part of any person's basic knowledge about the world, whether for travel or keeping track of events around the world.[1] When someone gives you directions, or asks them of you, the brain automatically attempts to draw a rudimentary map. Your mind may even see roads as lines and rivers as bands or buildings as small squares. Maps are, of course, also useful for understanding history and geography. Maps tell us about the physical and cultural aspects of the world, but they can be deceiving. Colors, for example, can be used to subtly suggest "good guys" or "bad guys." Countries can be made smaller or larger to suggest relative importance. Maps can be made deliberately incorrect—to confuse the "enemy."

Every map, therefore, has a point of view or perspective. It has an author (the cartographer), a subject, and a theme. The subject in this exercise book is Western Civilization; themes vary from boundaries to distribution of religious groups. The subject and theme represent the author's interest, but also his or her skills, political viewpoints, and historical context. Thus, maps do not represent reality, but a version of reality. Maps are like snapshots of the world, a moment in time and space with a definite historical context. One of the earliest maps in existence is from the Babylonians in the fifth century BC. In this map the Babylonians are situated precisely in the middle of the universe, all the rest radiated from them— their own perception of the world.

A world map from the 16th century show the continents as far as they were known to the Europeans during this age of discovery.[2] Compare a 16th century map to any later chart of the Americas and note how different in size and shape the continents are at different periods of time (clearly, the continents themselves did not change that much that quickly). The earlier world map reveals many things about the authors: their interests, their skills, and their knowledge of geography. One can see, from the examples of maps above, that the interest of the author is revealed by the selection of details for the map. In even the most "objective" map, one simply cannot add all details in all maps. The map would be rendered incomprehensibly complicated and useless.

---

[1] I would like to thank the undergraduate students in the History of Western Civilization courses at Northern Arizona University. They provided indispensable help and advice in the development of this workbook.

[2] The creation of maps has a complex and evolving history. It is a very ancient human activity -- the oldest known map, from ca. 5000 BC, was found in central Italy carved on a rock overlooking a Neolithic settlement.

To understand the basic appearance of a map, imagine the world as you see it from an airplane. The very straight lines that you see are generally roads and highways. The winding bands are rivers. Rectangles may be buildings and large dark green masses are forests. Cities are conglomerations of rectangles. If you simply took a picture from your airplane and had it printed you would have a photographic map: a reduced representation of a portion of the surface of the earth.

How we see the world from an airplane is, however, somewhat different from how we see it on a map. The world is round (most people agree). The map page is flat. All map makers, therefore, pick a perspective (as we have seen) and a scale from which to display their particular purpose or orientation. Many different scales of maps are used. That simply means that there are maps with different proportions between the distance on the map and the actual distance on the world. The larger the fraction (or proportion), the smaller the territory covered. Inches per mile or centimeters per kilometer are the most common kind of scale. The scale is merely a fraction comparing the measures on the map (inches or centimeters) with the measures on the ground (miles or kilometers).

Finding the exact location of any place requires several steps. Reproducing this location accurately is further complicated by the fact noted above: the world is round and most maps are not. This fact of life leads to unavoidable distortion in the spatial representation of locations. (You may notice that the shapes of continents change slightly from map to map. This is because the distortion is different depending upon the perspective of the map.) And flat maps are not likely to be completely superseded by globes. Carrying a globe on a hike or road trip would be very inconvenient.

Nevertheless, maps are becoming more and more accurate. Cartographers, especially since the Late Middle Ages, have worked to perfect map making. In order to make a map (or to read one) a frame of reference is chosen. A grid system within the frame of reference is usually used to help pinpoint locations on the map. In this exercise book the grid pattern has usually been removed in order to make the maps less cluttered, but normally the lines of latitude and longitude would be included on the map.

Map makers, in order to build a grid system, chose the north and south poles as two definite, and not arbitrary, points from which to begin dividing up the world. Midway between these poles a line was drawn around the world (this is the equator). Next, lines were drawn parallel to the equator up and down to each of the poles (the lines of latitude). To complete the grid lines were drawn from pole to pole (the lines of longitude).

The equator provides a natural line from which to measure, but there is no such natural longitude line (but one is put in by convention and is called the prime meridian). A longitudinal starting point is obviously needed as a point of reference. The line through Greenwich, England is now most commonly used, but many nations have created maps with their own most important cities as reference points. The United States made maps with Washington DC as the prime meridian. The Spanish drew their reference line through Madrid, the Greeks through Athens, the Dutch through Amsterdam and so on.

This particular exercise book is designed to help you understand the relation between places and people through time. Both maps and timelines are used to help you order events and historical locations. In order to make the maps less cluttered, there are no lines of longitude and latitude drawn in. All map exercises incorporate three parts. There is a brief introduction to each exercise. A locations section asks you to find and correctly place the number of a city, site or other feature or draw a boundary on the map. The questions section asks you to attempt to relate, or synthesize, some of the historical and geographical information that you have absorbed. This section expects you to answer in short essay form. The chronology exercises at the end of the workbook ask you to place events on a time line. This is intended to aid you in study and in the understanding of how events relate to one another temporally.

BRIEF BIBLIOGRAPHY

Demko, George with Jerome Agel and Eugene Boe. 1992. *Why in the World, Adventures in Geography*. New York: Doubleday. This is a fun and easy to read introduction to mapping and geography. It does an excellent job of pointing out the importance of geography.

Greenhood, David. 1964. *Mapping*. Chicago: University of Chicago Press. This book provides a clear and concise introduction to maps and mapping.

Wood, Denis. 1992. *The Power of Maps*. New York: The Guilford Press. In this book Wood shows how maps are used and abused. It is an excellent introduction to the way maps have been used by groups and individuals to make an argument or present a point of view.

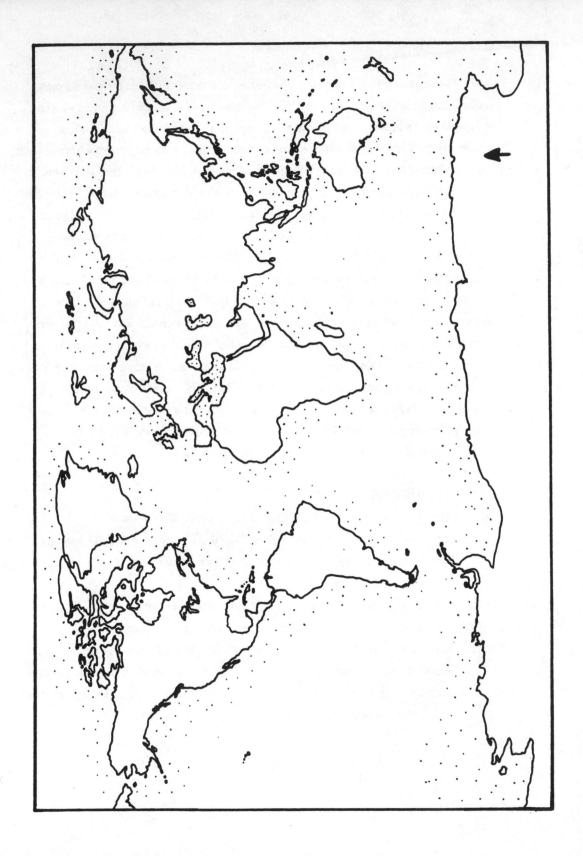

EXERCISE 1
The Geographical Context of the Mediterranean, Near East and Europe
(Use an historical atlas of your choice)

This exercise puts western Europe into perspective as just one part of the whole planet. "Western civilization" developed in a world context. It was not an isolated entity. Interactions among the various regions and people are evident from very early in human history. People traded with one another for food, tools and raw materials. In that process, they learned about one another, sometimes adopting practices, sometimes improving upon the technologies and customs that they found.

The earliest civilizations were found worldwide, in the valleys of the Fertile Crescent, India, China and Egypt. Western civilization can be traced to the early societies of the Near East and Egypt.

Locations

Place the numbers of the locations in the appropriate place and then, shading or drawing in, with different colored pencils, the following regions and geographical features.

A. Regions:

1. Anatolia
2. Arabia
3. Balkan Peninsula
4. Britain
5. China
6. Egypt
7. Fertile Crescent
8. Iberian Peninsula
9. Iran
10. North Africa
11. Russia

B. Rivers:

12. Danube
13. Euphrates
14. Nile
15. Rhine
16. Tigris

C. Seas and Oceans:

17. Atlantic
18. Black Sea
19. Indian Ocean
20. Mediterranean
21. North Sea

22. Pacific
23. Persian Gulf
24. Red Sea

D. Mountains:

25. Alps
26. Apennines
27. Caucasus
28. Pyrenees
29. Rockies
30. Taurus

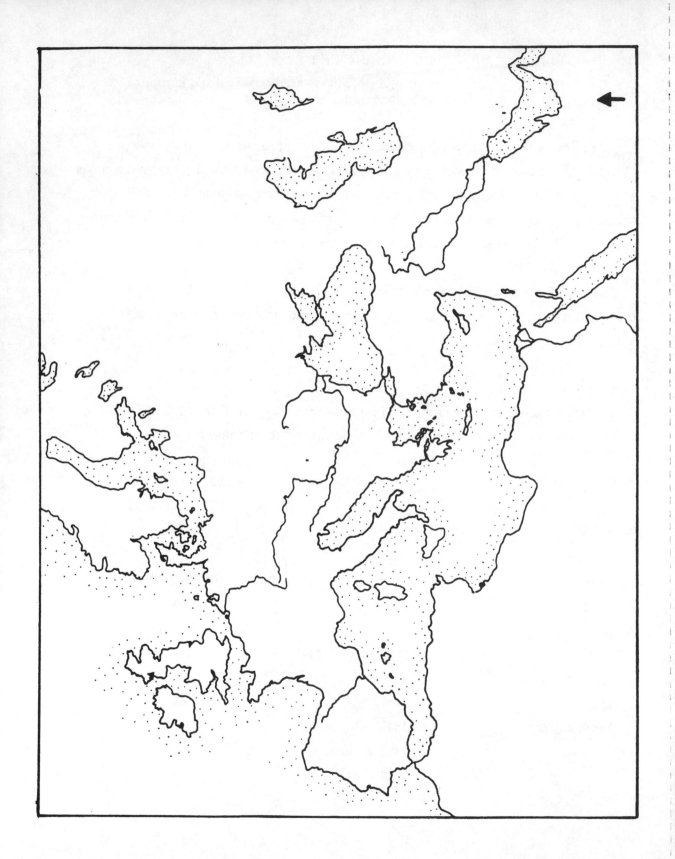

EXERCISE 2
The Era of Crisis: Black Death and War

The Black Death was a disaster of enormous magnitude. It killed from 25 to 50% of the population of Europe. In some cases entire villages were wiped out. Some cities saw their populations reduced by more than half. The inhabitants of Europe naturally responded to this disaster in a variety of inventive ways -- not all of them pleasant. The disaster had cultural, economic and religious results. Many wars were fought after the disease passed, in part because of the dislocation resulting from population loss and economic disruption.

Locations

With different colored pencils, trace the progression of the Black Death. Also place the numbers of the following cities and battle sites.

A. Approximate boundary of the disease:

1. In December 1347
2. In June 1348
3. In December 1348
4. In June 1349
5. In December 1349
6. In June 1350
7. In December 1350

B. Cities and battle sites:

8. Agincourt
9. Calais
10. Cologne
11. Crecy
12. Dublin
13. Durham
14. Hamburg
15. London
16. Messina
17. Milan
18. Paris
19. Rome
20. York

Questions

Discuss European responses to the Black Death. What were some of the psychological and religious responses experienced by the inhabitants of Europe? Give specific examples. What economic ramifications did the Black Death have? Be fairly detailed. In what ways did the Black Death have long term political effects?

By the fourteenth century Italy had a well established system of city-state governments, often in conflict with one another. By the fifteenth century there were only a few, very powerful states left. They vied with one another for a variety of reasons, often calling on the Papacy or the Holy Roman Empire of the Germans to support their claims. Frequent warfare was the result, and unification of Italy was a long way away. In contrast, Spain was home to several independent Christian nations that had managed, militarily, to take the peninsula from those practicing Islam-- in particular -- and Judaism. The Spanish enforced strict orthodoxy. Unlike the leaders and states of Italy, Isabella of Castile and Ferdinand of Aragon made major progress toward early unification of the Iberian peninsula. Their combined power and wealth, plus the support of the Catholic Church, would make them a real threat to countries near and far. This exercise considers the territories and states of both Spain and Italy.

Locations

With different colored pencils, place the number of the following cities on your map and number and shade or draw in the following political boundaries.

A. Italy:	7. Rep. of	13. Navarre	21. Madrid
1. Duc. of Ferrara	Florence	14. Portugal	22. Mantua
2. Duc. of Milan	8. Rep. of Siena		23. Milan
3. Duc. of	9. Rep. of Venice	**C. Cities:**	24. Naples
Modena		15. Barcelona	25. Poitiers
4. Duc. of Savoy	**B. Iberian**	16. Ferrara	26. Seville
5. Kingdom of	**Peninsula:**	17. Genoa	27. Toledo
Naples	10. Aragon	18. Lisbon	28. Trent
6. Papal States	11. Castile	19. Lucca	29. Valencia
	12. Granada	20. Lyons	30. Venice

Questions

Name the five major powers in Italy during the fifteenth century. How did these powers come to dominate? Why weren't they stable and peaceful? Also explain the emergence of the independent Christian states on the Iberian peninsula. Why were Ferdinand and Isabella so successful?

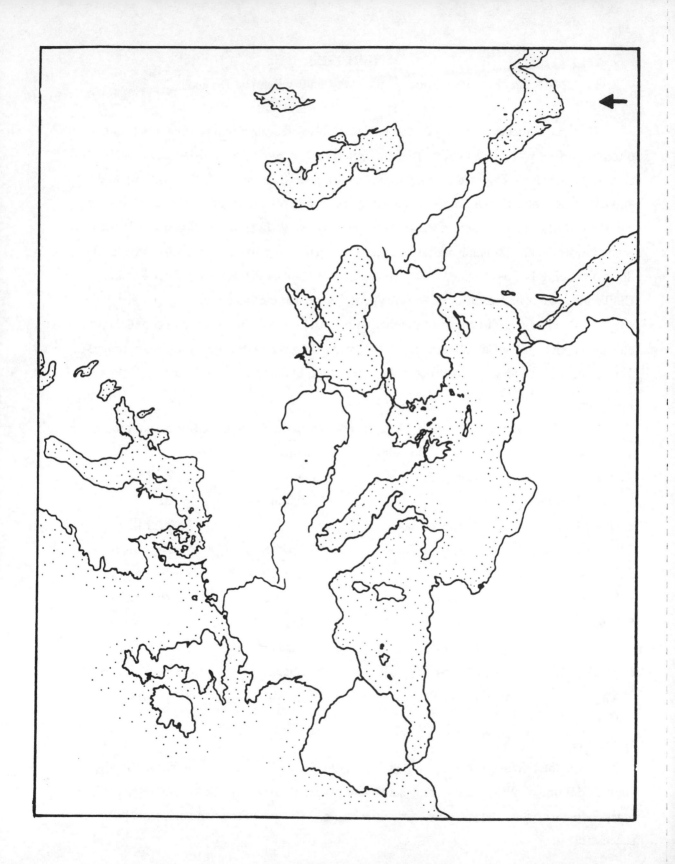

EXERCISE 4
Catholics and Protestants in 1550

In the sixteenth century abuses by the Catholic church, in particular the papacy, were reaching a crisis point. Many reform movements grew out of the frustration of the times, some made surprisingly influential by the dissemination of these new ideas through the written word, now easily spread because of the printing press. The Reformation in Germany was to be one of the most influential. This particular reform movement was led by Martin Luther, the founder of Lutheranism. It was not long before the population of Europe had chosen sides: Protestant (e.g. Lutheran, Calvinist, Anglican) or Catholic. This exercise identifies some of the divisions, by religion, that appeared in Europe by the mid sixteenth century.

Locations

On your map, place the number of the following cites and countries (using different colors lightly shade in the approximate territory of the countries)in its proper location on the map. Next to each number, write in the local religion.

A. Cities:

1. Antwerp
2. Cologne
3. Dublin
4. Edinburgh
5. Geneva
6. Lisbon
7. London
8. Munich
9. Nuremberg
10. Paris
11. Prague
12. Rome
13. Seville
14. Trent
15. Vienna
16. Wittenberg
17. Zurich

B. Countries:

18. Denmark
19. Norway
20. Sweden

Questions

Compare and contrast the Reformation in England and Germany. Were the same reforming factors at work? Who initiated the Reformation in England? In Germany? What impact did the Reformation generally have on society in Europe? Give several examples.

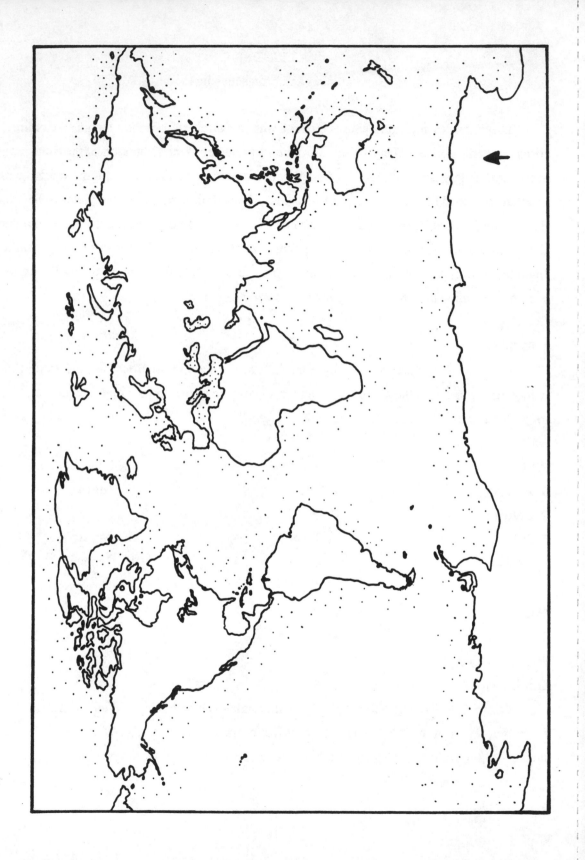

The sixteenth and seventeenth centuries were dominated by war and socio-economic crises. In the midst of this, however, Europeans made unprecedented expansion into other parts of the world. These new frontiers provided opportunities to exploit and convert local populations and the Europeans soon realized the economic advantages of doing so. Since European states had achieved the technological know-how and wealth needed to make regular forays beyond their borders, the pace of conquest and exploitation was rapid. And this had dramatic consequences for the conquered peoples.

Locations

On your map, place the number of the following cities in its proper location on the map. Next to each number, write in whether the city is independent, or controlled by the Spanish or Portuguese.

A. Cities

1. Bahia
2. Calicut
3. Canton
4. Elmina
5. Lima

6. Manila
7. Mozambique
8. Ormuz
9. Tenochtitlan
10. Zanzibar

Questions

Summarize the development of the Portuguese maritime empire. What motivated the first Portuguese explorers? What routes did they take in their early travels? Similarly, summarize Spanish explorations. What motivated the Spanish explorers?

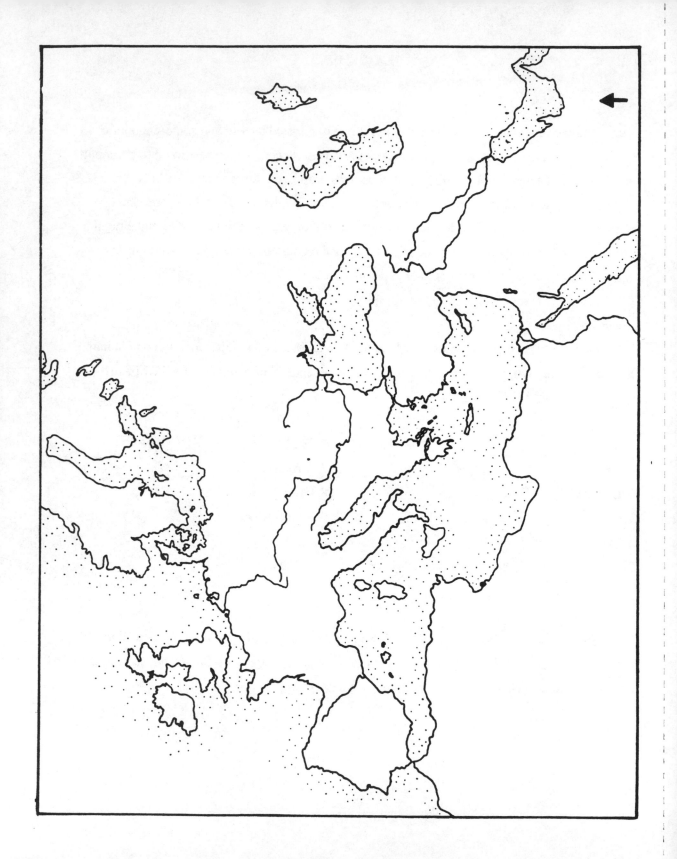

EXERCISE 6
The Ottoman Empire

The Turkish people, led by the Ottomans, conquered the Byzantine Empire once and for all in 1453 with the capture of Constantinople. This was a tremendous victory and afterwards the Turks were on the move. They added vast tracts of lands to their wealthy empire.

The Ottomans were very effective at getting the Europeans to accept them as an equal power. They had a very intricate and effective government, with a strong and well organized military. This exercise traces the growth of Ottoman strength and influence in Europe and the Mediterranean regions.

Locations

With different colored pencils draw and number the boundaries of the Ottoman Empire. Also place the numbers of the following cities and regions correctly on your map.

A. Boundaries:

1. Ottoman Empire at 1451
2. Ottoman Empire at 1481
3. Ottoman Empire at 1521
4. Ottoman Empire at 1566

11. Lepanto
12. Mohács
13. Palermo
14. Tunis
15. Vienna

B. Cities and sites:

6. Athens
7. Belgrade
8. Cairo
9. Damascus
10. Istanbul

C. Regions:

16. Anatolia
17. Egypt
18. Moldavia
19. Syria
20. Transylvania

Questions

After 1566 the northern boundaries of the Ottoman empire were fairly fixed. What occurred to stop further movement into Europe? What were the strengths and weaknesses of the Ottomans? What were (are) the long term results of their conquests?

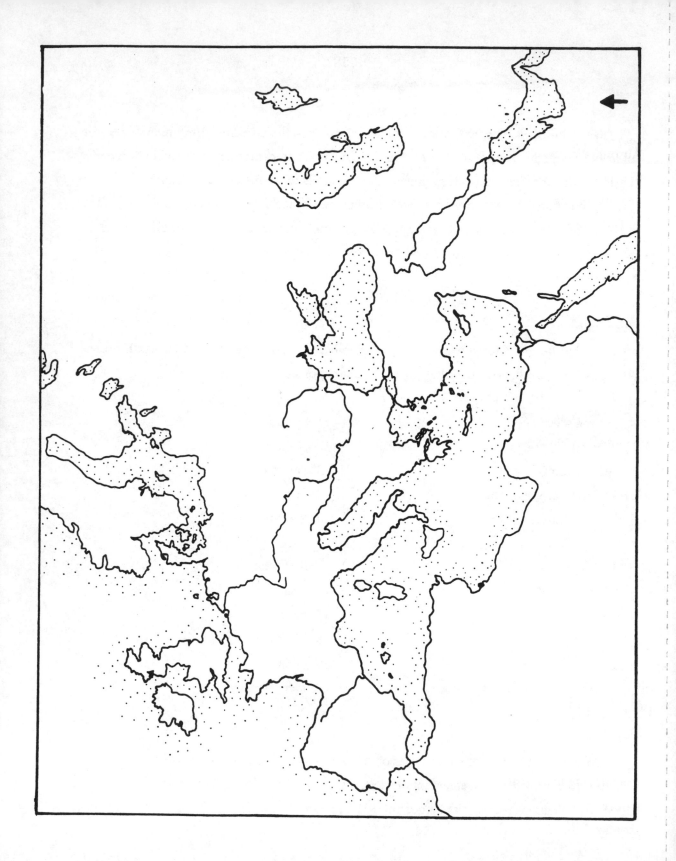

After the Reformation swept Europe a system of secular states began to appear. Absolutist monarchs tried to stabilize the boundaries and societies of the European states. After the end of the Thirty Years' War, however, Germany was still made up of more than three hundred independent states, each vying for power and territory. The Holy Roman Empire was an entity in name only. Out of the hundreds of German states, two became most powerful: Brandenburg and Austria. Both of these states would grow and strengthen because of particularly dominating families, the Hohenzollerns and the Hapsburgs respectively.

The boundaries and peoples of these regions of (especially middle and eastern) Europe were mobile and unstable. This exercise is intended to give you an idea for how these European people were settled in this era.

Locations

With a colored pencil number and draw the boundaries (with as much accuracy as possible) for the following states and regions. Please place the seventeenth or eighteenth century date of the boundary that you draw next to the number that you place on the map. On your map, also place the number of the following cities in its proper location.

A. States:	7. Silesia	12. Slovenia	17. Dresden
1. Austria		13. Transylvania	18. Nuremberg
2. Bosnia	**B. Regions:**		19. Prague
3. Croatia	8. Bohemia	**C. Cities:**	20. Vienna
4. France	9. Moldavia	14. Breslau	
5. Galacia	10. Prussia	15. Budapest	
6. Hungary	11. Saxony	16. Cracow	

Questions

What were the long term goals of the Hohenzollern dynasty? How successful were they in achieving their goals? Also describe the Austrian government in this era. What factors made it develop as it did? Why did the Hapsburgs decide to move into more eastern territories and abandon the thought of a purely German empire?

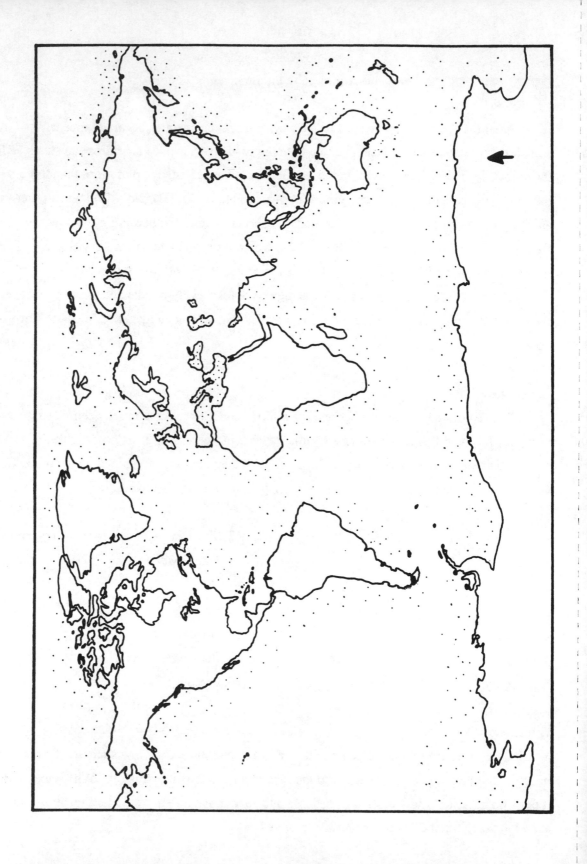

The European states of the eighteenth and early nineteenth centuries were characterized by growth and rivalries. These rivalries were not all played out on European territory. The main powers became very interested in the concept of a balance of power throughout the world. This meant they felt the need to limit the power of some states and expand and support the power of others, both near and far. The tools used for this process were mainly two: diplomacy and the military. Foreign ministries sprouted in far off places and the sizes of standing armies were increased. Maritime powers increased the sizes of their navies.

Countries which were not at the same level of industrial development were claimed for their natural resources and people by the European powers. This exercise looks at the European territories of this era, as well as some of the uses and abuses put to them.

Locations

On the world map provided, number, outline and lightly shade in, using different colors, the following empires (from about 1783) and regions. Leave in white the areas unclaimed by the Europeans or the Ottomans.

A. Empires:

1. British Empire
2. Dutch Empire
3. French Empire
4. Ottoman Empire
5. Portuguese Empire
6. Russian Empire
7. Spanish Empire

B. Regions

8. Guinea
9. Mexico
10. Philippines

Questions

The colonial empires varied in their structures and means of exploitation. Compare and contrast the French and British colonies generally, and specifically in North America. Why were the British ultimately more successful in North America than the French?

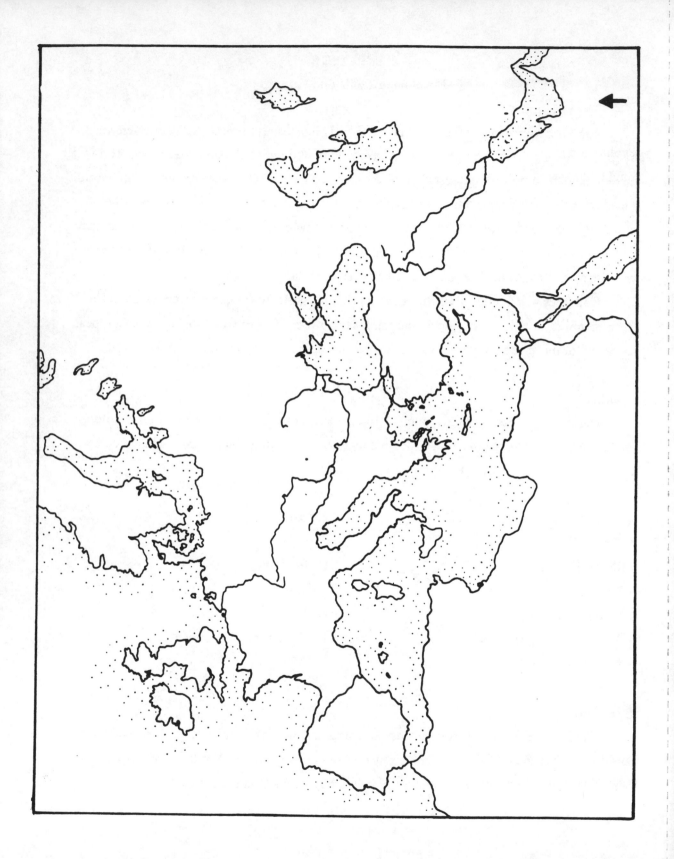

The late eighteenth century saw two important revolutions in the west: the American revolution and the French revolution. Both were the result of long term problems. The French sought, like the Americans, to ground their constitution in the idea of equal rights. The implementation of equal rights was neither easy nor peaceful. Other European nations feared that violent upheaval would spread from France and, thus, an informal coalition formed against the French. In response, the French had built up a large and impressive army and conquered even the Netherlands.

Terror, instability and confusion soon dominated French politics and the economy. This situation allowed Napoleon to stage the coup d'état that would bring him to power. With his power he would try to create a long-lasting European empire, enlightened and fair. This exercise traces the growth of the French state in Europe.

Locations

With different colored pencils number and outline the boundaries of the French Republic and its satellites. Next, in different colors, number and draw the boundaries of the French Empire under Napoleon as well as those territories under French control. Also number and correctly place the following cities and sites on your map.

A. Boundaries:

1. French Republic
2. French satellites during the Republic
3. French Empire
4. Areas under Napoleonic French control
5. Areas allied to Napoleonic France

B. Cities and battle sites:

6. Austerlitz
7. Leipzig
8. Marseilles
9. Paris
10. Waterloo

Questions

Napoleon's empire did not last long. Why not? What factors ultimately led to Napoleon's rise and fall? More generally what were the results of the revolutions of the eighteenth century? What were some of the major social, political, and territorial changes?

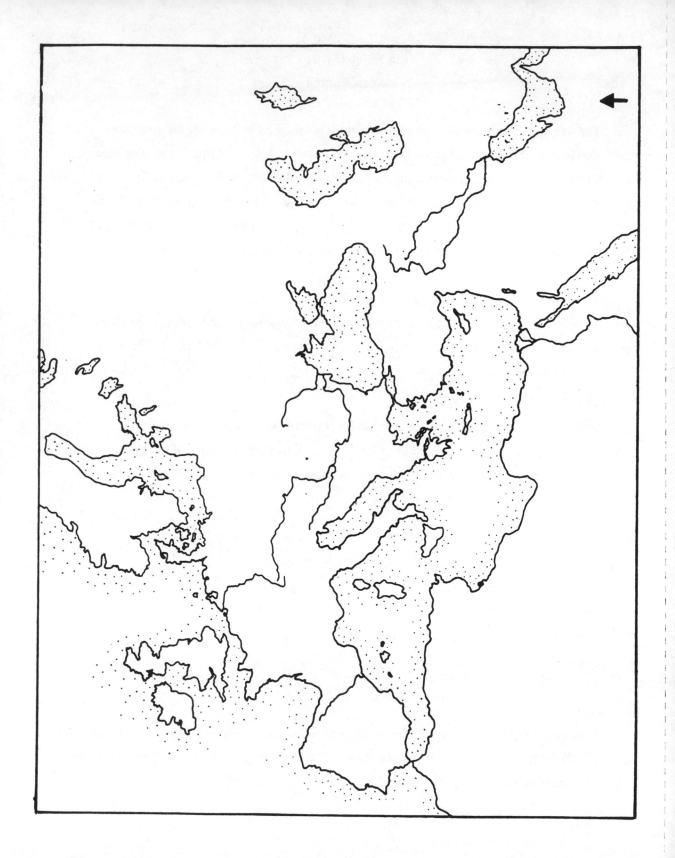

Following the peace settlement known as the Congress of Vienna (1815), a measure of territorial stability was restored to the continent. In many cases old monarchies and elites were re-established in power. Peace arrangements were made in an attempt to contain revolutionary forces unleashed in the late eighteenth century. Such attempts would prove to be futile in the long run. This exercise provides a familiarity with the nations of the early nineteenth century and the areas that would suffer revolts in the middle of the nineteenth century.

Locations

With colored pencils number and draw the boundaries of the following nations. Then correctly place the numbers of the following selection of battle sites (from revolutions of 1848-1849) on your map.

A. Nations in 1815:	7. Spain	13. Cracow
1. Denmark	8. Switzerland	14. Florence
2. France	9. The Papal States	15. Frankfurt
3. Great Britain		16. Milan
4. Kingdom of the Two	**B. Battle sites of 1848:**	17. Munich
Sicilies	10. Baden	18. Palermo
5. Netherlands	11. Berlin	19. Prague
6. Portugal	12. Budapest	20. Rome

Questions

Briefly describe the problems that the conservative movement had in containing the forces for change. What role did Metternich play in these conservative attempts to maintain order? What effect did the ideology of Liberalism have on the development of revolutionary movements? And what effect did the ideology of Nationalism have on the development of revolutionary movements?

The revolutions that freed North America had little immediate effect on the colonial status of countries in South and Central America. These lands remained in the hand of European powers into the nineteenth century. The Spanish and the Portuguese held these territories and were loath to give up their wealth, even though their powers were weakening. Slowly the lands of South America demanded and got independence, despite the Spanish use of well trained troops to crush the resistance.

Locations

With colored pencils number, draw the boundaries and provide the date of independence for the following nations of South and Central America. Correctly place the numbers of the following sites on your map.

A. Nations:

1. Argentina
2. Bolivia
3. Brazil
4. Chile
5. Columbia
6. Costa Rica
7. Ecuador

8. El Salvador
9. Guatemala
10. Honduras
11. Nicaragua
12. Paraguay
13. Peru
14. Uruguay
15. Venezuela

B. Cites:

16. Bogatá
17. Buenos Aires
18. Lima
19. Rio de Janeiro
20. Santiago

Questions

Which Latin American states failed to gain their independence at this time (1845)? What role did the United States play in movement for independence in Latin America? Why did the United States become involved?

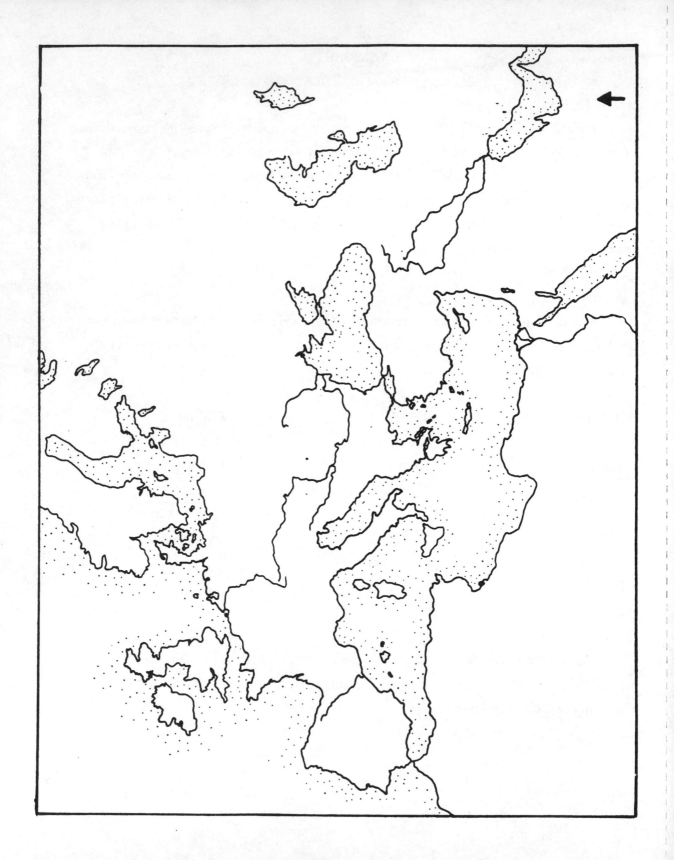

Despite attempts to maintain the status quo, a new wave of revolution and reform spread across Europe in the second half of the nineteenth century. Again the French took a leading role. The 1830's to the 1850's saw revolts in Spain, Portugal, France, Italy, Russia and Poland. By the 1870's the map of Europe had changed.

Locations

On the map provided draw the boundaries of and number the following European states, regions and cities as of 1871.

A. States:

1. Austria-Hungary
2. Belgium
3. Denmark
4. France
5. German Empire
6. Great Britain
7. Greece
8. Italy
9. Ottoman Empire
10. Spain
11. Switzerland

B. Regions:

12. Albania
13. Bosnia
14. Croatia-Slovenia
15. Serbia

C. Cities:

16. London
17. Madrid
18. Paris
19. Rome
20. Vienna

Questions

Succinctly explain the processes by which Italy and Germany became unified. What main factors allowed them to unify? In what ways were these processes similar, and in what ways were they different?

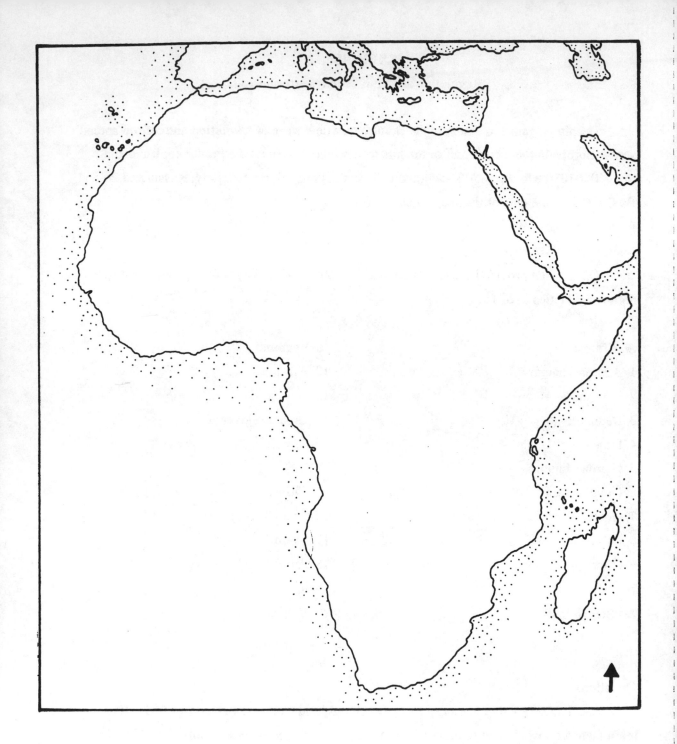

In the latter years of the nineteenth century European states were again interested in overseas expansion. The Americas were lost to them so these states turned their attentions particularly to Asia and Africa. They were not, however, able to dominate the territories in Asia and Africa quite as successfully as they had done in earlier centuries. These new colonies were nevertheless worth all the trouble as they provided many immediate benefits, both material and social.

Locations

Africa was carved up among the Europeans, with only Ethiopia and Liberia as independent nations. With different colored pencils, color in and number the territories claimed by the European states (remember each number may appear more than one time). Then properly draw in and/or place the numbers of the following African regions and geographical features on your map. There will be overlap.

A. European colonies:	B. Regions/independent states	C. Geographical features:
1. Belgium		
2. Boer Republic	8. Algeria	16. Atlantic Ocean
3. France	9. Angola	17. Indian Ocean
4. Germany	10. Congo	18. Mediterranean Sea
5. Great Britain	11. Egypt	19. Niger River
6. Italy	12. Ethiopia	20. Nile River
7. Portugal	13. Kenya	
	14. Liberia	
	15. Madagascar	

Questions

What were the benefits (economic, social, political) of African colonies to the Europeans? Briefly, what were some of the effects of this colonialism on the continent of Africa? Why were Liberia and Ethiopia able to remain independent?

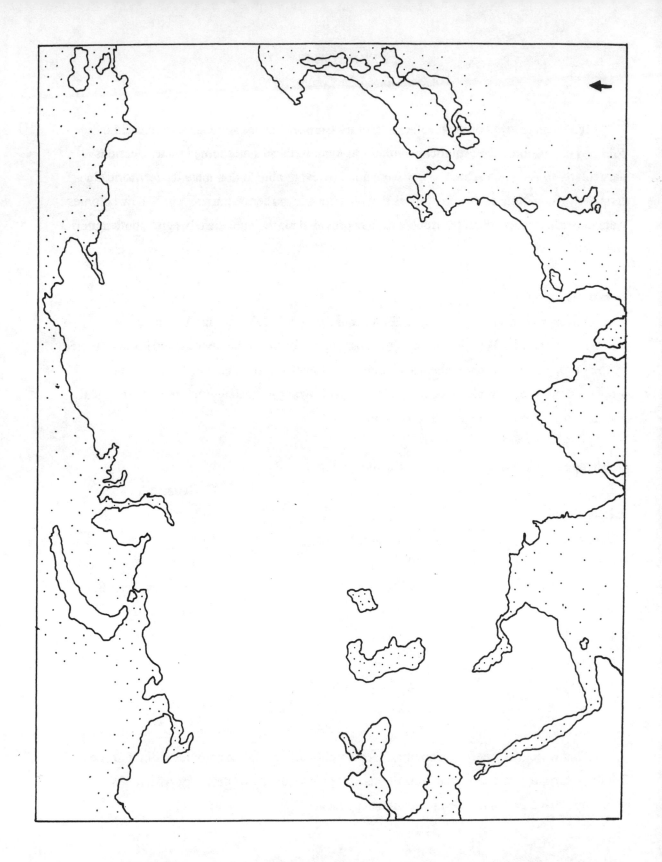

peans. Some territories were acquired by the

e of the western powers. The United States

and claimed some territory for themselves.

be superior to the Asian and African people,

by explaining that such oppression was of

Burden" exemplifies this western feeling of

, shade in and number the possessions or

wers. Also properly place the number the

s

15. Persia

16. Philippines

C. Cites:

17. Bangkok

s

18. Beijing

19. Bombay

20. Saigon

ndent? How did they manage to remain so?

interests in Asia. What attracted each to the

act? With what results for the people of Asia?

Crises in the Balkans have been a common occurrence over the centuries. The Austrians had held Bosnia and Herzegovina under their protection until 1908 when the states were formally annexed. The Serbs, because their hopes for a larger Serbian kingdom were dashed, helped precipitate a international incident in response to Austrian actions. In 1912 more attention was drawn to the region when the Ottoman Turks were defeated in the First Balkan war. New divisions of territories resulted. 1913 saw another Balkans war and further divisions of the Balkans. This exercise traces the divisions of the Balkans prior to World War I.

Locations

With different colored pencils outline and number the boundaries of the Balkan states after the Congress of Berlin in 1878 and in 1913.

A. Boundaries 1878 (use dotted lines)

1. Greece
2. Macedonia
3. Serbia

B. Boundaries 1913 (use solid lines)

4. Albania

5. Austria-Hungary
6. Bulgaria
7. Greece
8. Montenegro
9. Romania
10. Serbia

Questions

What were the goals and motivations of the Serbians in the Balkan wars? Were they successful in reaching their goals? What were the long-term results of the Balkan Wars?

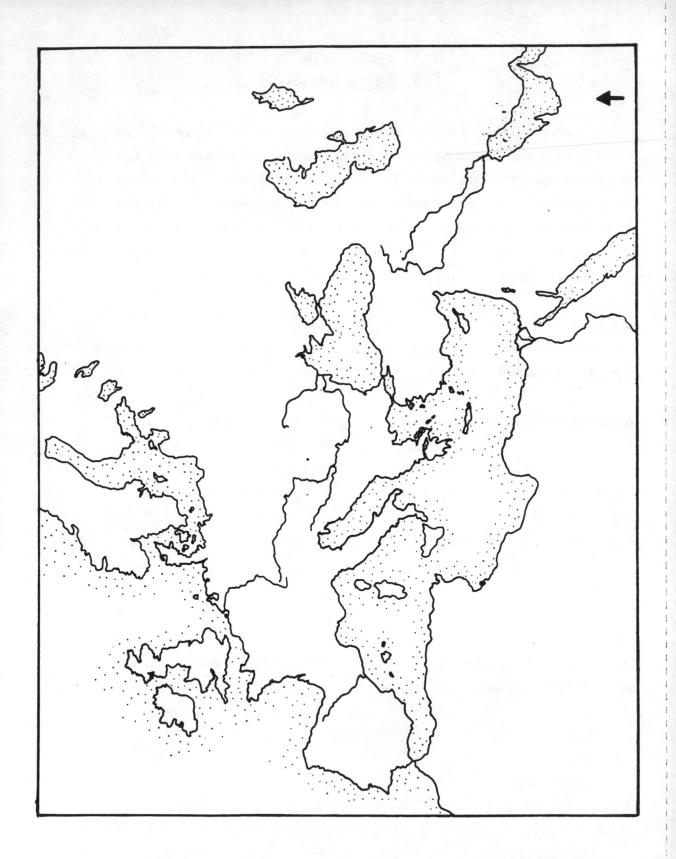

World War I was one of the defining events of the twentieth century. The brutality, overwhelming scope and length of the war, and its final settlement would prepare the road for yet another major conflict. Its destructiveness was a shock and disappointment to Europeans, intellectual, industrial worker and farmer alike. Not surprisingly, the conflict was ignited by a confrontation between Austria and Serbia, after the heir to the Austrian throne was assassinated in Sarajevo, a Bosnian city. This exercise compares the political divisions of Europe before and after the "Great War."

Locations

On the map provided draw and number the approximate boundaries of pre-World War I Europe for the following states. Next draw and number the boundaries of the following states after the end of the war. Also properly place the number the following cities on your map.

A. Boundaries of pre-World War I Europe (use dotted lines)		B. Boundaries of post World War I Europe (use solid lines)	
1. Albania	6. Germany	16. Albania	22. Hungary
2. Austria-Hungary	7. Greece	17. Austria	23. Poland
3. Belgium	8. Italy	18. Bulgaria	24. Romania
4. Bulgaria	9. Montenegro	19. Czechoslovakia	25. Yugoslavia
5. France	10. Netherlands	20. France	C. Cities:
	11. Romania	21. Germany	26. Belgrade
	12. Russia		27. Berlin
	13. Serbia		28. London
	14. Spain		29. Paris
	15. Switzerland		30. Warsaw

Questions

Explain the process by which the war was widened to include combatants such as the Ottomans and the United States. What was the social impact of the war on Europeans? What result did this war have on European political and economic dominance of world affairs?

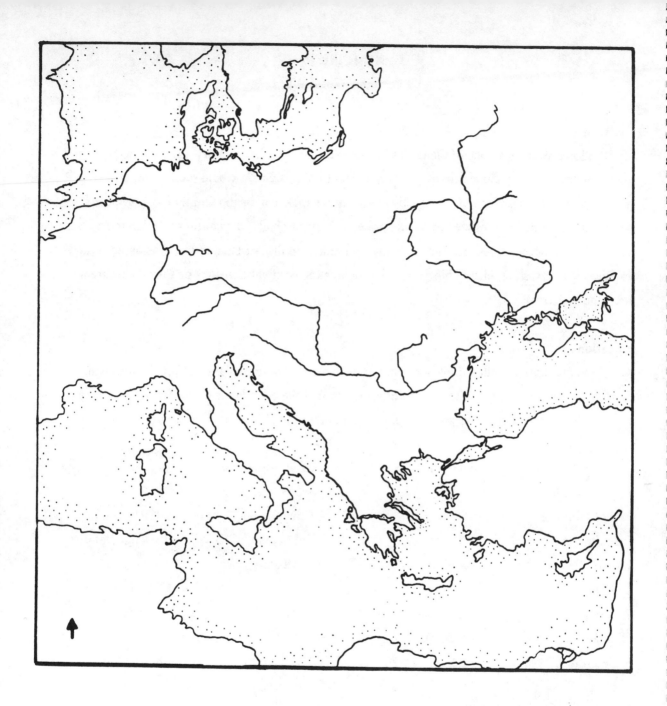

Asia, too, received the attentions of the Europeans. Some territories were acquired by the Europeans, others came strongly under the influence of the western powers. The United States also evinced an interest in the Pacific rim countries and claimed some territory for themselves.

Western people generally felt themselves to be superior to the Asian and African people, and thus easily justified their imperialistic attitude by explaining that such oppression was of mutual benefit. Kipling's poem the "White Man's Burden" exemplifies this western feeling of superiority.

Locations

On the map provided, using colored pencils, shade in and number the possessions or spheres of influence for the following imperial powers. Also properly place the number the following regions and cities on your map.

A. Colonial possessions

1. Dutch
2. France
3. Germany
4. Great Britain
5. Japan
6. Portugal
7. Russia

8. United States

B. Regions

9. Ceylon
10. China
11. East Indies
12. India
13. Japan
14. Korea

15. Persia
16. Philippines

C. Cites:

17. Bangkok
18. Beijing
19. Bombay
20. Saigon

Questions

Which Asian territories remained independent? How did they manage to remain so?

Compare and contrast British and Russian interests in Asia. What attracted each to the region? How did the Russians and British interact? With what results for the people of Asia?

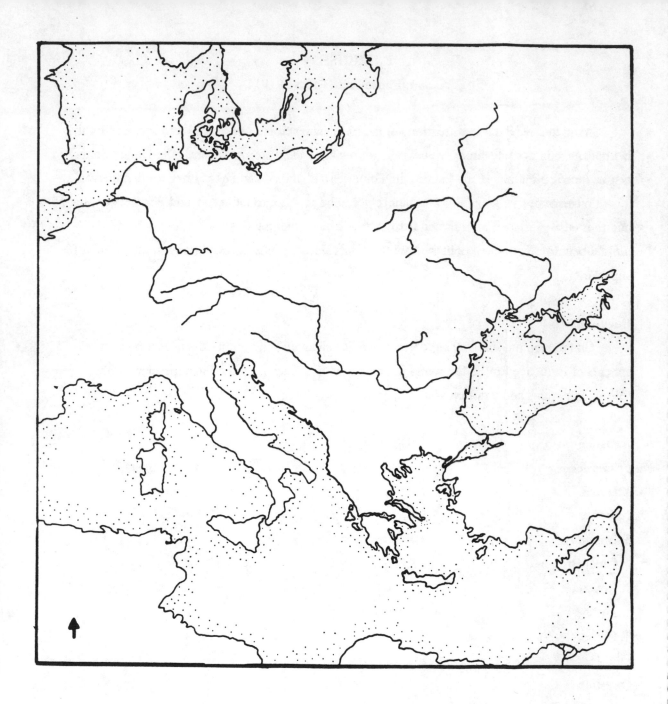

Crises in the Balkans have been a common occurrence over the centuries. The Austrians had held Bosnia and Herzegovina under their protection until 1908 when the states were formally annexed. The Serbs, because their hopes for a larger Serbian kingdom were dashed, helped precipitate a international incident in response to Austrian actions. In 1912 more attention was drawn to the region when the Ottoman Turks were defeated in the First Balkan war. New divisions of territories resulted. 1913 saw another Balkans war and further divisions of the Balkans. This exercise traces the divisions of the Balkans prior to World War I.

Locations

With different colored pencils outline and number the boundaries of the Balkan states after the Congress of Berlin in 1878 and in 1913.

A. Boundaries 1878 (use dotted lines)

1. Greece
2. Macedonia
3. Serbia

B. Boundaries 1913 (use solid lines)

4. Albania

5. Austria-Hungary
6. Bulgaria
7. Greece
8. Montenegro
9. Romania
10. Serbia

Questions

What were the goals and motivations of the Serbians in the Balkan wars? Were they successful in reaching their goals? What were the long-term results of the Balkan Wars?

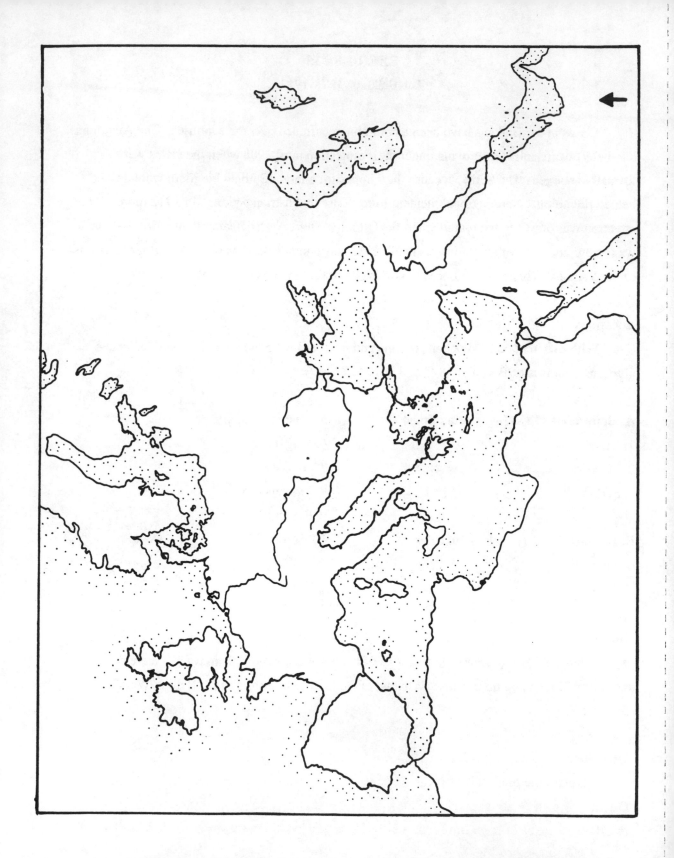

EXERCISE 16
Europe after World War I

World War I was one of the defining events of the twentieth century. The brutality, overwhelming scope and length of the war, and its final settlement would prepare the road for yet another major conflict. Its destructiveness was a shock and disappointment to Europeans, intellectual, industrial worker and farmer alike. Not surprisingly, the conflict was ignited by a confrontation between Austria and Serbia, after the heir to the Austrian throne was assassinated in Sarajevo, a Bosnian city. This exercise compares the political divisions of Europe before and after the "Great War."

Locations

On the map provided draw and number the approximate boundaries of pre-World War I Europe for the following states. Next draw and number the boundaries of the following states after the end of the war. Also properly place the number the following cities on your map.

A. Boundaries of pre-World War I Europe (use dotted lines)		B. Boundaries of post World War I Europe (use solid lines)	
1. Albania	6. Germany	16. Albania	22. Hungary
2. Austria-Hungary	7. Greece	17. Austria	23. Poland
3. Belgium	8. Italy	18. Bulgaria	24. Romania
4. Bulgaria	9. Montenegro	19. Czechoslovakia	25. Yugoslavia
5. France	10. Netherlands	20. France	**C. Cities:**
	11. Romania	21. Germany	26. Belgrade
	12. Russia		27. Berlin
	13. Serbia		28. London
	14. Spain		29. Paris
	15. Switzerland		30. Warsaw

Questions

Explain the process by which the war was widened to include combatants such as the Ottomans and the United States. What was the social impact of the war on Europeans? What result did this war have on European political and economic dominance of world affairs?

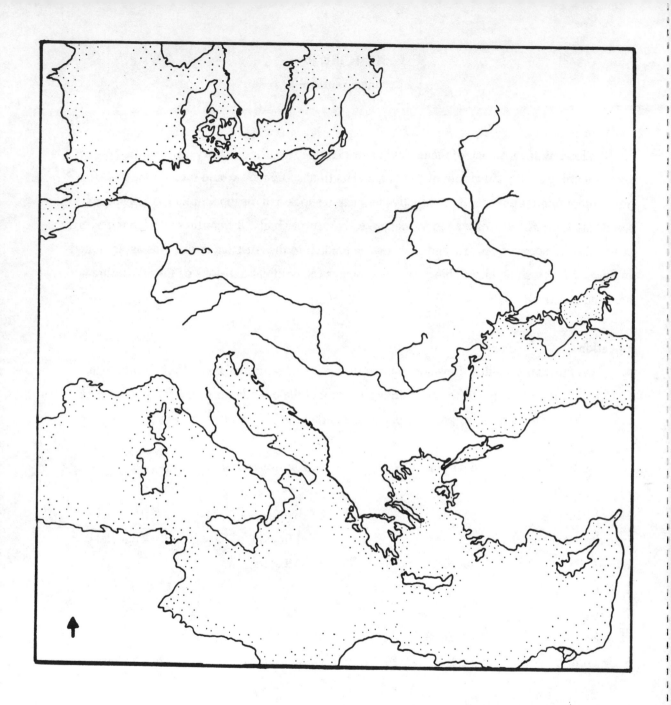

In 1919 Europeans were optimistic, despite early signs of serious economic trouble foreshadowing the Great Depression. Deeply affected by their financial setbacks and plunged into poverty, the Germans came to resent their position in the post war world. According to a contemproray observer, Heinrich Hauser, "An almost unbroken chain of homeless men extends the whole length of the great Hamburg-Berlin highway..."

The depressed economy helped precipitate non-democratic political solutions to economic problems and the creation of authoritarian and totalitarian states. World War II was inevitable when one such power, the Nazi party, ignited a form of German nationalism that proclaimed, among other things, a need for more living space (*lebensraum*). Once again a massively destructive war was fought on European soil, with devastating demographic, material, and psychological results. Here we look at one result: the territorial settlement of Central Europe (where the greatest changes occurred) following the war.

Locations

On the map provided, number and draw in the new boundaries of Central Europe after World War II. Next, shade in the approximate areas of the Allied influence that existed after the war in Germany. Also shade in all the territory gained by the Soviet Union. Mark with a dotted line and number the "Iron Curtain" that went up after 1955.

A. Boundaries
1. Czechoslovakia
2. Germany
3. Hungary
4. Poland
5. White Russia

B. Zones in Germany and acquired territory
6. British
7. French
8. Soviet
9. US
10. Territory gained by the Soviet Union

11. "Iron Curtain"

C. Cities:
12. Berlin
13. Bern
14. Brussels
15. Bucharest
16. Milan
17. Munich

18. Rome
19. Vienna
20. Warsaw

Questions

How long was Germany divided into Zones? Describe the division of Berlin. What territory was lost to Germany and to whom did it go? Territorially, who gained the most from the settlement after World War II?

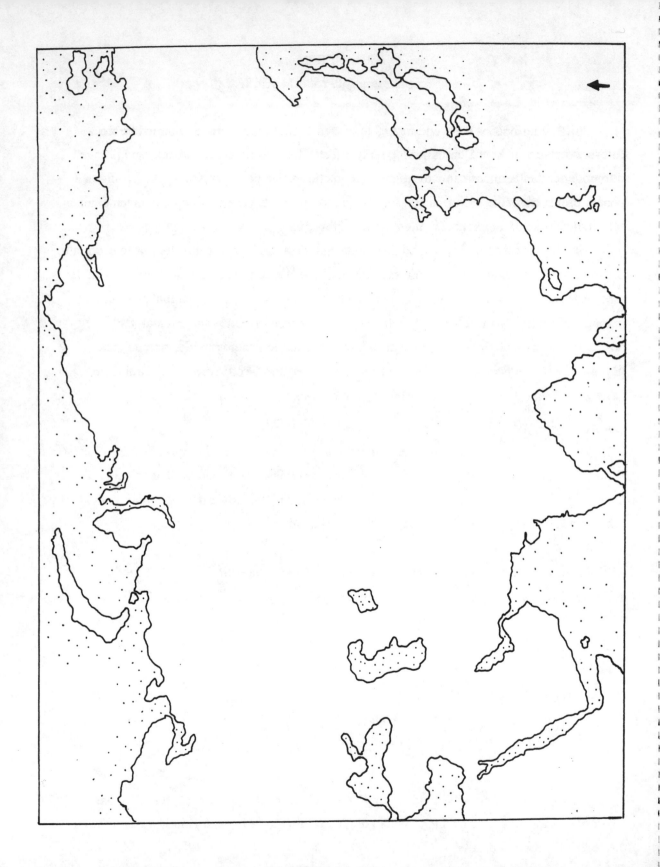

World War II had a profound impact in the territories influenced and claimed by the European powers in Africa, Asia and the Middle East. The colonies made claims for independence and nationalistic movements were enthusiastically embraced. In Asia and the Middle East successful revolutionary attempts added up. India and Pakistan freed themselves from British rule. Other Asian countries also managed to loosen the bonds of European control. In the Middle East, the growing nationalism of the Arabs helped put an end to colonial control, but the Arabs were unable to prevent the creation of a new Jewish state, Israel.

Locations

On the map provided, using different colored pencils, number, draw the approximate boundaries and provide the date of independence for the following states of the Middle East and Asia.

A. Boundaries

1. Bangladesh

2. Cambodia

3. India

4. Iraq

5. Israel

6. Jordan

7. Kuwait

8. Philippines

9. Syria

10. Vietnam

Questions

What factors generally encouraged the collapse of the European colonial empires? what role did nationalism play in the growing independence movements?

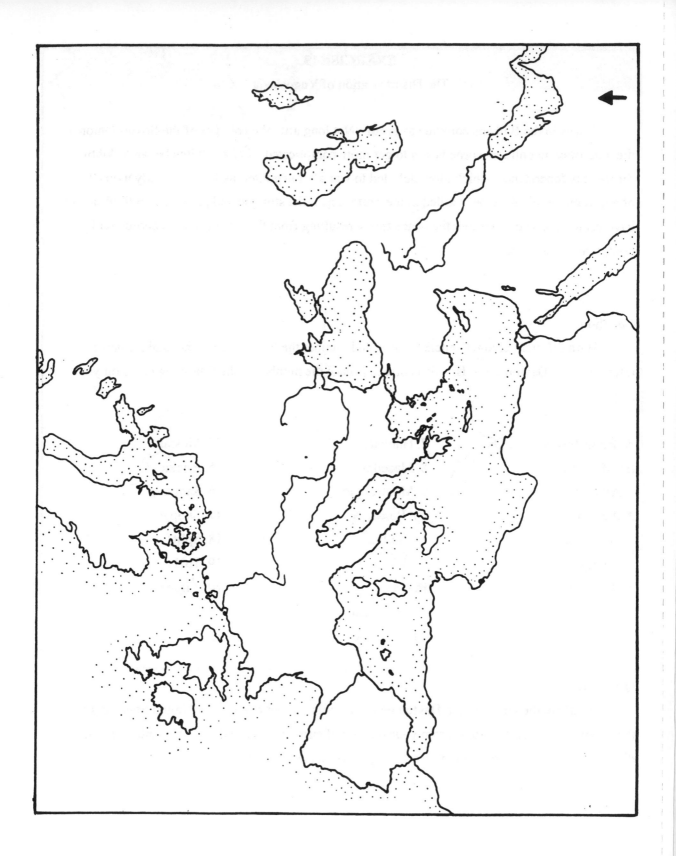

EXERCISE 20
The Future of Europe: Political and Cultural Boundaries

You have seen state boundaries change continually over time. This is an exercise of your imagination. On the map provided draw the boundaries of Europe as you believe they will be fifty years from today. Mark on your map major changes in population that you predict (do you think large numbers of, for example, ethnic Croats will move to another country or countries?). Do you believe there will be any more major wars on the order of the first and second world wars? Why or why not? What effect will the current Balkan crisis have in the long run?

Next justify your predictions. Why do you believe the changes you suggest will occur? Use both current and past events to support your position.

AD 1066	Battle of Hastings
1073-1085	Pope Gregory VII
1077	Absolution of Henry at Canossa
1079	Peter Abelard born
1096-1099	The First Crusade
1098-1179	Hildegard of Bingen
1122	Concordat of Worms
1135	Maimonides born in Spain
1139	Portugal established
1142	Death of Peter Abelard
1170	Thomas Becket murdered
1152-1190	Frederick I Barbarosssa of Germany
1162-1227	Genghis Khan and the rise of the Mongols
1187	Saladin conquers Jerusalem
1204	Christian sack of Constantinople
1215	Magna Carta
1220-1292	Roger Bacon
1226	Death of St. Francis of Assisi
1266	Charles of Anjou invades Italy
1290	Expulsion of the Jews from England
1291	Surrender of Acre
1302	First Estates General in France
1305	Avignon Papacy begins
1321	Death of Dante
1337	Hundred Years' War begins
1340	Birth of Chaucer
1347	The Black Death arrives
1378	The Great Schism begins
1431	Death of Joan of Arc
1445-1450	The birth of printing
1452-1519	Leonardo da Vinci
1453	Fall of Constantinople to the Ottoman's; end of the Hundred Years' War
1469	Marriage of Ferdinand of Aragon and Isabella of Castile
1469-1492	Lorenzo d'Medici rules Florence
1471-1528	Albrecht Dürer
1475-1564	Michelangelo
1492	Expulsion of Jews from Spain; Columbus
1502	Expulsion of Muslims from Spain
1511	*In Praise of Folly* by Erasmus
1517	Luther's Ninety-Five Theses
1572	St. Bartholomew's Day Massacre
1588	The Spanish Armada
1598	Edict of Nantes

CHRONOLOGY 2
Early Modern Europe: AD 1600-1800

AD 1565-1642	Galileo
1614	Death of Shakespeare
1622-1673	Molière
1623-1704	John Locke
1630	Death of Johannes Kepler
1642	Birth of Isaac Newton
1648	Independence of the United Provinces; Peace of Westphalia
1651	Hobbes' *Leviathan* published
1660	Restoration Monarchy -- Charles II
1661-1715	Reign of Louis XIV
1683	Turkish siege of Vienna
1689	English Bill of Rights
1697-1698	Peter the Great visits the West
1712	Steam Engine first used
1739-40	Hume, *Treatise of Human Nature*
1740-1748	War of the Austrian Succession
1748	Montesquieu published *The Spirit of the Laws*
1756-1763	The Seven Years' War
1772	First Partition of Poland
1773	Pugachev's Rebellion
1776	American Declaration of Independence
1776-1788	Gibbon, *Decline and Fall of the Roman Empire*
1787	Power Loom invented
1789	Fall of the Bastille
1791	American Bill of Right's adopted
1792	Abolition of the French Monarchy
1794	Execution of Robespierre
1799	Napoleon as First Consul

CHRONOLOGY 3
Modern Europe: AD 1800 to the Present

AD 1804-1815	Emperor Napoleon I
1814	Exile of Napoleon to Elba
1815	Battle of Waterloo
1821	Death of Napoleon
1821-1832	The Greek Revolt
1823	Monroe Doctrine
1825	Decembrist Revolt
1829	Treaty of Adrianople
1834	Poor Law in Great Britain
1840-1926	Claude Monet
1848	Revolution in Germany; Revolutions in Italy
1851	World's first industrial fair
1863	Emancipation Proclamation
1871	German Empire is Proclaimed; Darwin's *Descent of Man* appeared
1879-1953	Josef Stalin
1894-1917	Tsar Nicholas II of Russia
1896	Ethiopians defeat the Italians
1899-1902	Boer War
1912-1913	Balkan Wars
1914	Assassination of Archduke Ferdinand of Austria
1916	Murder of Rasputin
1917	Russian Revolution
1918-1921	Russian Civil War
1923	Beer Hall Putsch led by Adolph Hitler
1929	Death of Freud
1933	New Deal in the United States
1934	Hitler sole ruler in Germany
1938	*Kristallnacht*; Germany annexes Austria
1939	Britain and France declare war on Germany
1945	Death of Mussolini; Germany surrenders; Hitler commits suicide; Atomic bomb dropped on Japan; Japan surrenders
1949	NATO formed; Simone de Beauvoir published *The Second Sex*
1955	Warsaw Pact
1961	Berlin Wall is built
1964-1973	Vietnam War
1968	Student Revolts in Paris
1979	USSR invades Afghanistan; French legalize abortion
1990	Germany reunified
1991	Failed Coup in USSR; disunion spreads